D1308086

WG

The Salesman's
Book of Wisdom

The Salesman's Book of Wisdom

Timeless Principles of
Effective Salesmanship

Compiled and Edited by Criswell Freeman

WALNUT GROVE PRESS
Nashville, TN 37205

ISBN 1-887655-83-2

The ideas expressed in this book are not, in all cases, exact quotations, as some have been edited for clarity and brevity. In all cases, the author has attempted to maintain the speaker's original intent. In some cases, material for this book was obtained from secondary sources, primarily print media. While every effort was made to ensure the accuracy of these sources, the accuracy cannot be guaranteed. For additions, deletions, corrections or clarifications in future editions of this text, please write WALNUT GROVE PRESS.

Printed in the United States of America
Typesetting & Page Layout by Sue Gerdes
Editor for Walnut Grove Press: Alan Ross
2 3 4 5 6 7 8 9 10 • 99 00 01 02

ACKNOWLEDGMENTS
The author gratefully acknowledges the helpful support of Angela Freeman, Dick and Mary Freeman, and Mary Susan Freeman.

For Dad

My Favorite Salesman

Table of Contents

A Note to the Reader

You hold in your hand a book of quotations that summarizes the principles of effective salesmanship. The ideas on these pages, if put into practice, will improve not only your sales results but also your life.

For over thirty years, I have studied and practiced the art of selling. At the age of fourteen, I attended my first sales course; my eyes were opened to the vast opportunities awaiting the enthusiastic salesperson. During a fifteen-year career in real estate, I owned companies that bought and sold over a billion dollars in properties.

In midlife, I answered an inner calling to study psychology. The more I learned about human nature, the more I became convinced that the principles of effective selling are also the principles of healthy living. A good salesperson is honest, empathic, hard-working, organized and persistent. These traits, not surprisingly, also lead to success outside the workplace.

If you're a salesman (and I use that term to signify both men and women), congratulations. You've chosen a rewarding career that offers boundless potential. But even if you don't earn your living as a professional salesperson, read on. Because whether you know it or not, you're in sales. It's a requirement of the human condition.

1

The Joy of Selling

Selling has been called the greatest profession in the world and with good cause. Few experiences in business can match the excitement of a big sale. But the thrill of the close is always preceded by mundane activities such as training, prospecting and preparation. For the successful salesman, there is no dozing before the closing.

What keeps top sales professionals motivated? In part, it is the love of selling. Effective salespeople love to make calls. Ineffective salespeople love *the idea* of selling, but they dislike the act of making the call. The results are predictable.

Legendary football coach Vince Lombardi warned, "If you aren't fired with enthusiasm, you'll be fired with enthusiasm." His words apply not only to professional football players but also to professionals in all fields. So if you wish to become an exceptional salesman, remember that sales calls should be savored, not endured. Once you learn to love your work, your work will love you back.

We are all salesmen every day of our lives.

Charles M. Schwab

Everyone lives by selling something.

Robert Louis Stevenson

Nothing happens until somebody sells something.

Sales Adage

If you're not selling your product ...
don't blame the product.

Estée Lauder

As salesmen, we are personal service
corporations, and the only thing we have
to sell is our time.

Brian Tracy

When you sell on commission,
you own your own business.

Thomas J. Watson

Business has only two
basic functions —
marketing and innovation.

Peter Drucker

Even if you build a better
mousetrap, you've still
got to sell it.

Ross Perot

Each day provides its own gifts.

Martial

Each day comes bearing its own gifts.
Untie the ribbons.

Ruth Ann Schabacker

The clearest sign of wisdom
is continued cheerfulness.

Montaingne

Seeds of discouragement will not grow
in the thankful heart.

Anonymous

Happiness is a habit. Cultivate it.

Elbert Hubbard

Thanksgiving invites God to bestow
a second benefit.

Robert Herrick

Finding your particular talent or vocation
is the first step in the art of being successful.

Conrad Hilton

Happiness is not a state to arrive at
but a manner of traveling.

Samuel Johnson

The finest test of character is seen in the
amount and the power of gratitude we have.

Milo H. Gates

The best way to be thankful is to use
the gifts the gods provide you.

Anthony Trollope

As one gets on in years, there is a satisfaction
in doing a thing for the sake of doing it.

Russell Conwell

Write on your heart that every day
is the best day of the year.

Ralph Waldo Emerson

Thanksgiving is a sure index
of spiritual health.

Maurice Dametz

2

Attitude

W. Clement Stone once observed, "There is very little difference in people, but that little difference makes a big difference: The little difference is attitude." It's no coincidence that Mr. Stone was one of the premier insurance salesmen of his day. He understood that positive thinking is the common denominator of successful people in general and successful salespeople in particular.

The fastest way to tune up any sales career is to perform an attitude adjustment. Attitude may seem like a little thing, but in selling it's everything.

I rate enthusiasm even above professional skill.
Sir Edward Appleton

The real secret of success is enthusiasm.
Yes, more than enthusiasm, I would say
excitement. I like to see people get excited.
When they get excited they make a success
of their lives.
Walter Chrysler

The world belongs to the enthusiast
who keeps cool.
William McFee

I prefer the errors of enthusiasm
to the indifference of wisdom.
Anatole France

Be enthusiastic.
Every occasion is an
opportunity to do good.

Russell Conwell

The mind is its own place and
can make a heaven of hell, a hell of heaven.

John Milton

Life reflects your own thoughts back to you.

Napoleon Hill

Most people are about as happy as they
make up their minds to be.

Abraham Lincoln

God gave you a gift of 86,400 seconds today.
Have you used one to say "thank you"?

William Arthur Ward

There is no duty so much underrated
as the duty of being happy.
Robert Louis Stevenson

A merry heart doeth good like a medicine.
Proverbs 17:22

As is our confidence, so is our capacity.
William Hazlitt

All things are possible to him that believeth.
Mark 9:23

Selling is essentially a transference of a feeling.

Zig Ziglar

Before a salesman sells
anything to anyone,
he must first sell it
to himself.

Napoleon Hill

Do not build up obstacles in your imagination.
Difficulties must be studied and dealt with,
but they must not be magnified by fear.

Norman Vincent Peale

Your business is never really good or bad
"out there." Your business is either good or bad
right between your two ears.

Zig Ziglar

Believe in yourself. Have faith in your abilities.
Without a humble but reasonable confidence
in your own powers, you cannot be successful
or happy.

Norman Vincent Peale

A positive mind tunes in
to other positive minds.

Napoleon Hill

Enthusiasm increased my income 700%.

Frank Bettger

Always bear in mind that
your own resolution to
succeed is more important
than any one thing.

Abraham Lincoln

Self-image sets the
boundaries of individual
accomplishment.

Maxwell Maltz

Nothing is more valuable to a man
than courage.

Terence

The thing we fear we bring to pass.

Elbert Hubbard

We must face what we fear; that is the case
of the core of the restoration of health.

Max Lerner

The best part of health is a fine disposition.

Ralph Waldo Emerson

Of all base passions, fear is most accursed.

William Shakespeare

Fear strikes out.

Pete Rose

The only security is courage.

La Rochefoucauld

What a new face courage puts on everything!

Ralph Waldo Emerson

Feelings of confidence depend upon the type
of thoughts you habitually occupy. Think
defeat, and you are bound to be defeated.

Norman Vincent Peale

We are more often frightened than hurt,
and we suffer more from imagination
than from reality.

Seneca

As a rule, what is out of sight disturbs
men's minds more than what they see.

Julius Caesar

The happiness of your life depends upon
the quality of your thoughts; therefore,
guard accordingly.

Marcus Aurelius

A good disposition is a virtue in itself,
and it is lasting.

Ovid

No one keeps up his enthusiasm automatically.
Enthusiasm must be nourished with new actions,
new aspirations, new efforts, new vision.
It is one's own fault if his enthusiasm is gone;
he has failed to feed it.

Papyrus

Practice being excited.

Bill Foster

A cloudy day is no match
for a sunny disposition.

William Arthur Ward

If you're not happy every morning when you get up and leave for work, you're not going to be successful.

Donald M. Kendall

All that we are is the result of what we have thought. The mind is everything. What we think, we become.

Buddha

Worry is a form of fear, and all forms of fear produce fatigue. A man who has learned not to feel fear will find the fatigue of daily life enormously diminished.

Bertrand Russell

A person with a negative mental attitude can sell nothing. He may take an order, but no selling was done.

Napoleon Hill

3

Hard Work

The world remembers Thomas Edison as an inventor, but he was also a spectacular salesman. Edison understood that simply inventing a product, no matter how useful, was not enough. He knew that he also had to sell his product to the public. And he did.

Like any good salesman, Edison was an energetic worker. In fact, he attributed his success not to intellect but to diligence. He once said, "Genius is 1% inspiration and 99% perspiration." The same ratio applies in sales.

The only place where success comes before work is in the dictionary.

Vidal Sassoon

Selling is the easiest job
in the world if you work
it hard, but it's the
hardest job in the world
if you work it easy.

Frank Bettger

Luck is not chance. It's toil.
   Fortune's expensive smile is earned.

Emily Dickinson

If there is no wind, row.

Latin Proverb

The great composer does not set to work
because he is inspired but becomes inspired
because he is working. Beethoven, Wagner,
Bach and Mozart settled down day after day
to the job in hand with as much regularity
as an accountant settles down each day
to his figures. They didn't waste time
waiting for inspiration.

Ernest Newman

Iron rusts from disuse. Stagnant water loses
its purity. So does inaction sap the vigors of
the mind.

Leonardo da Vinci

The most unhappy of all men is the man who cannot tell what he is going to do, has got no work cut out for him in the world, and does not go into it. For work is the grand cure of all the maladies and miseries that ever beset mankind — honest work, which you intend getting done.

Thomas Carlyle

The greatest value lies not in getting things done but in doing them.

W. T. Grant

The great end of life is not knowledge but action.

Thomas Henry Huxley

The highest reward for man's toil is not what he gets for it but what he becomes by it.

John Ruskin

When we accept tough jobs as a challenge
to our ability and wade into them with joy
and enthusiasm, miracles can happen.
When we do our work with a dynamic,
conquering spirit, we get things done.

Arland Gilbert

To bring one's self to a frame of mind and
to the proper energy to accomplish things
that require plain hard work continuously
is the one big battle that everyone has.
When this battle is won for all time,
then everything is easy.

Thomas A. Buckner

Energy, even like the Biblical grain
of mustard seed, will move mountains.

Hosea Ballou

I'm a great believer in luck, and I find the harder
I work, the more I have of it.

Thomas Jefferson

God helps them who help themselves.

Poor Richard's Almanac

If you believe in the Lord,
He will do half the work: the last half.

Cyrus Curtis

Well done is twice done.

Poor Richard's Almanac

If you want a thing done well, do it yourself.

Napoléon I

If you don't want to do something,
one excuse is as good as another.

Yiddish Saying

To be disciplined from within, where all
is permissible, where all is concealed —
that is the point.

Montaigne

When trouble comes, wise men take
to their work.

Elbert Hubbard

Problems are only opportunities
in work clothes.

Henry Kaiser

Doubt, of whatever kind, can be ended
by action alone.

Thomas Carlyle

Never despair, but if you do,
work on in despair.

Edmund Burke

It's the job that's never started that takes
longest to finish.

J. R. R. Tolkien

There is nothing so fatal to character
as half-finished tasks.

David Lloyd George

All the beautiful sentiments in the world
weigh less than a single lovely action.

James Russell Lowell

He who desires but acts not
breeds pestilence.

William Blake

If you want to conquer
fear, don't sit home
and think about it.
Go out and get busy.

Dale Carnegie

Action is worry's worst enemy.

Old-Time Saying

One today is worth two tomorrows.

Ben Franklin

The shortest answer is doing.

George Herbert

God gives talent.
Work transforms
talent into genius.

Anna Pavolva

Work keeps you alive.
You'll rust faster than
you'll wear out.

Harland Sanders

4

Goals

Clearly defined goals are an integral part of selling. Sales offices have quotas for the same reasons that schools have grades: measurement and motivation. So if you're looking for a sure-fire way to motivate yourself, begin by writing down a clearly defined set of objectives.

Personal goals should be challenging but attainable — and measurable. Once your goals are safely on paper, review them often. You'll discover that clearly defined objectives pay a double dividend: Not only are you motivated to achieve your goals, but when you do, you'll know.

Make no little plans;
they have no magic
to stir the blood.

Daniel H. Burnham

When your company sets quotas, set yourself a still bigger quota.

Thomas J. Watson

Make a success of living by seeing the goal
and aiming for it unswervingly.

Cecil B. DeMille

Without some goal and some effort to reach it,
no man can live.

Fyodor Dostoyevsky

Not failure, but low aim, is the crime.

James Russell Lowell

Hell is to drift, heaven is to steer.

George Bernard Shaw

Enthusiasm for one's goal lessens
the disagreeableness of working toward it.

Thomas Eakins

Where we stand is not as important
as the direction in which we are moving.

Oliver Wendell Holmes, Jr.

My interest is in the future because I am
going to spend the rest of my life there.

Charles F. Kettering

The ultimate function of prophecy
is not to tell the future but to make it.

W. W. Wagar

The tragedy of life doesn't lie in not reaching your goal. The tragedy lies in having no goal to reach.

Benjamin E. Mays

Decide exactly what you want in life, write it down in detail, and decide that you will pay the price to achieve it.

Brian Tracy

A goal is a dream with a deadline.

Harvey Mackay

Begin with an intense burning desire for something definite.

Napoleon Hill

Nothing will come of nothing.
Dare mighty things.

William Shakespeare

In the long run we only hit what we aim at.
Aim high.

Henry David Thoreau

We aim above the mark to hit the mark.
Every act has some falsehood
or exaggeration in it.

Ralph Waldo Emerson

If you would hit the mark, you must aim
a little above it.

Henry Wadsworth Longfellow

The method of the enterprising is to plan
with audacity and execute with vigor.

Christian Bovee

When you reach for the stars you may not
make it, but you won't come up with
a handful of mud either.

Leo Burnett

Great minds have purposes.
Others have wishes.

Washington Irving

If you would create something,
you must *be* something.

Goethe

First say to yourself what you would be;
then do what you have to do.

Epictetus

How many cares one
loses when one decides
not to be something
but to be someone.

Coco Chanel

Follow your desire as long as you live;
we should not lessen the time of following
desire, for the wasting of time
is an abomination to the spirit.

Ptahhotep

I like dreams of the future better
than the history of the past.

Thomas Jefferson

The best way to make your dreams
come true is to wake up.

Paul Valéry

Whatever course you have chosen for
yourself, it will not be a chore but an adventure
if you bring to it a sense of the glory of striving,
if your sights are set far above the merely
secure and mediocre.

David Sarnoff

Nobody ever drew up his plans for life so
well but what the facts and the years
and experience always introduce
some modification.

Terence

It is a bad plan that admits no modification.

Publilius Syrus

Admire those who attempt great things,
even if they fail.

Seneca

The plans of the diligent lead to profit.

Proverbs 21:5

Arriving at one goal is the starting point of another.

John Dewey

Never run out of goals.

Earl Nightingale

Hold yourself responsible for a higher
standard than anyone else expects of you.
Never excuse yourself.

Henry Ward Beecher

Great things are done when man
and mountain meet.

William Blake

It's not the mountain we conquer,
but ourselves.

Sir Edmund Hillary

5

The Customer

The purpose of every business is the same: to find and serve a customer. Thus, the customer should, by rights, be the primary focus of all businesses. In poorly run companies, the customer is viewed as an interruption or a dollar sign ... nothing more. Such attitudes endanger the very existence of these companies.

If you seek to build your business — and especially if that business is sales — remember that your job is, in essence, an exercise in finding and serving people. And when it comes to your business, remember this simple poem:

The Customer

The more you find, and the more you serve,
The more you earn, and the more you deserve!

W. C. F.

Earning a customer's friendship
is far more vital and necessary than getting
his dollar today.

Milton S. Florsheim

You don't build a business
unless people come back.

Ralph Lauren

Make sure your work and your money
benefit someone besides yourself.

Napoleon Hill

The best-run companies stay as close
as possible to their customers.

Tom Peters

Satisfied customers
are the best advertisements.

Sales Adage

Give them quality.
That's the best kind
of advertising.

Milton S. Hershey

There is never a good sale for Neiman-Marcus
unless it's a good buy for the customer.

Herbert Marcus

The generous trader needs no scales.

Lao-tzu

If rascals knew the advantages of virtue,
they would become honest.

Ben Franklin

All virtue is summed up in dealing honestly.

Aristotle

Nothing astonishes men so much
as common sense and plain dealing.
Ralph Waldo Emerson

No man is more cheated than the selfish man.
Henry Ward Beecher

Don't compromise yourself.
You're all you've got.

Janis Joplin

Good selling is honest selling.

Napoleon Hill

The way you see people is the way you
treat them, and the way you treat them
is what they become.

Goethe

There's only one way to meet a dissatisfied
customer: head on!

George M. Kahn

We are not here merely to make a living.
We are here to enrich the world, and we
impoverish ourselves if we forget this errand.

Woodrow Wilson

There is only one way under high Heaven
to get anybody to do anything. Did you ever
stop to think of that? Yes, just one way.
And that is by making the other person
want to do it.

Dale Carnegie

Think as little as possible about yourself and
as much as possible about other people.

Eleanor Roosevelt

If you give them something worth paying for,
they'll pay.

Tom Peters

Never forget a customer.
Never let a customer
forget you.

Frank Bettger

6

The Presentation

In 1914, Thomas J. Watson, was named president of the company that would come to be known as IBM. Mr. Watson was not only a founding father of the computer industry, he was also a master salesman. And he had this practical advice about sales presentations. Watson said, "Don't worry about being a 'natural salesman.' Just get into an office or store or home and try to sell with sincerity."

If you're not a "natural salesman," a sales presentation can be a nerve-racking experience, unless you learn to worry more about the customer's needs than your own. But once you learn to "sell with sincerity," you'll forget about your own nervousness and close more sales. The next time you're making a sales presentation, be sincere, keep your thoughts focused on the customer's needs and above all, be yourself. When you do so, you'll discover this truth: In selling, sincerity breeds prosperity.

Remember, you're selling customer benefits,
not technology or product features.

George M. Kahn

Remember, you're not selling products
or services. You're selling solutions
to your customers' problems.

Robert L. Shook

A good sales presentation starts logically
and ends emotionally.

Zig Ziglar

In our factory, we
make lipstick. In our
advertising, we sell hope.

Charles Revson

Be fully prepared for your sales call.
It's a big confidence booster.

Ross Perot

The real salesman must sell something
of himself with each sale.

Robert W. Woodruff

It takes two people to make an argument, and
the salesman should never be one of them.

Thomas J. Watson

Never "pan" a competitor's product.
You cause the prospect to think
negative thoughts.

Napoleon Hill

Praise your competitors.

Frank Bettger

Easy always does it. Don't press.

Norman Vincent Peale

Throughout every presentation,
I assume the sale.

Joe Girard

As I grow older, I pay less attention
to what men say. I just watch what they do.

Andrew Carnegie

Truly outstanding salespeople
are excellent listeners.

Joe Girard

People ought to listen more slowly!

Jean Sparks Ducey

Listen with sincerity.

Joe Girard

There is only one rule for being a good talker
— learn how to listen.

Christopher Morley

To listen is an effort, and just to hear
is no merit. A duck also hears.

Igor Stravinsky

Speak the customer's language.

Sales Adage

Reading buying signals is an acquired skill.
So acquire it.

Joe Girard

See things from the other person's point of
view and talk in terms of his wants and needs.

Frank Bettger

To be able to ask a question clearly is
two-thirds of the way to getting it answered.

John Ruskin

Be simple.

Alfred E. Smith

Your enthusiasm will be infectious, stimulating and attractive to others. They will love you for it. They will go *for* you and *with* you.

Norman Vincent Peale

If you have an important point to make, don't try to be subtle or clever. Use a pile driver. Hit the point once. Then come back and hit it again. Then hit it a third time — a tremendous whack.

Sir Winston Churchill

Find the customer's key issue, then concentrate on it.

Frank Bettger

Ask yourself this question:
Would you buy from you?

Zig Ziglar

7

Persistence

Benjamin Disraeli observed, "The secret of success is constancy of purpose." Salesmen take note. The secret of sales success is consistency. The salesperson who sells every day of his working life enjoys a tremendous advantage over the salesman who sells only when the spirit moves him.

Exceptional salespeople make their calls every day, regardless of circumstances. Selling is an exercise in perseverance. It is a battle of attrition in which only the persistent survive and conquer. And to the victors go the sales.

Great things are not done by impulse but
by a series of small things brought together.

Vincent van Gogh

The secret of success is constancy of purpose.

Benjamin Disraeli

Press on: Nothing in the world can take
the place of perseverance.

Calvin Coolidge

This business of selling narrows down
to one thing, just one thing: seeing the people.

Walter LeMar Talbot

If you have a good idea, you have to keep
going back and keep marketing it — you've got
to keep calling on the prospects.

Ross Perot

You're only really working
when you're face-to-face
with a customer.
Everything else
is only prelude.

Brian Tracy

Plodding wins the race.

Aesop

Patience is a necessary ingredient of genius.

Benjamin Disraeli

Patience is a bitter plant,
      but it has sweet fruit.

German Proverb

God helps those who persevere.

The Koran

Patience is power; with time and patience,
      the mulberry leaf becomes silk.

Chinese Proverb

We do not meet with success except
by reiterated efforts.

Françoise de Maintenon

Diligence overcomes difficulties;
sloth makes them.

Ben Franklin

Failure is the path of least persistence.

Old-Time Saying

A wise man will make more opportunities
than he finds.

Francis Bacon

Perhaps perseverence has been the radical
principle of every truly great character.

John Foster

Patience and diligence, like faith,
      move mountains.

William Penn

Every noble work is at first impossible.

Thomas Carlyle

Patience and time do more than strength
      or passion.

La Fontaine

I walk slowly, but I never walk backwards.

Abraham Lincoln

It does not matter how slowly you go
      so long as you do not stop.

Confucius

He conquers who endures.

Persius

It is fatal to enter any war without the will to win it.

General Douglas MacArthur

We will either find a way or make one.

Hannibal

Victory belongs to the most persevering.

Napoléon I

Never, never, never give up.

Sir Winston Churchill

With ordinary talent and extraordinary perseverance, all things are attainable.

Sir Thomas Buxton

He who labors diligently need never despair; for all things are accomplished by diligence and labor.

Menander

There is no royal road to anything. Do one thing at a time and all things in succession. That which grows slowly, endures.

Josiah G. Holland

The block of granite, which is an obstacle in the pathway of the weak, becomes a stepping-stone in the pathway of the strong.

Thomas Carlyle

I am not the smartest or most talented person in the world, but I succeeded because I kept going, and going, and going.

Sylvester Stallone

It takes 20 years to make
an overnight success.

Eddie Cantor

Genius is nothing but a greater aptitude
for patience.

Ben Franklin

Hold on; hold fast; hold out.
Patience is genius.

Comte de Buffon

Endurance is nobler than strength and
patience nobler than beauty.

John Ruskin

Have patience with all things, but first of all
with yourself.

Saint Francis of Sales

Press on. Nothing in the world can take the place of perseverance. Talent will not; nothing is more common than unsuccessful men with talent. Genius will not; unrewarded genius is almost a proverb. Education will not; the world is full of educated derelicts. Persistence and determination alone are omnipotent.

Calvin Coolidge

Diligence is the mother of good luck, and God gives all things to industry.

Ben Franklin

In everything worth having, even in pleasure, there is a point of pain or tedium that must be survived so that the pleasure may revive and endure.

G. K. Chesterton

There is no great achievement that is not the result of patient working and waiting.

Josiah G. Holland

The secret is this:
    Strength lies solely in tenacity.
Louis Pasteur

We can do anything we want if we stick to it
    long enough.
Helen Keller

Our greatest weakness lies in giving up.
    The most certain way to succeed is
    to always try just one more time.
Thomas Alva Edison

It's hard to beat a person who never gives up.
Babe Ruth

What do you do when you feel discouraged? Make one more call.

George M. Kahn

There is no need for a salesman to ponder whether to start forward with his left foot or his right. All he has to do is get going and keep going toward the place where the prospect is.

Thomas J. Watson

8

Rejection

Rejection is an inevitable consequence of selling. Ironically, this fact is good news for the disciplined salesperson. If personal rejection were not an integral component of the sales process, *anyone* could sell; superior salesmen would be commonplace. But the reality is this: Superior salesmen are quite uncommon and thus demand a high premium in the marketplace.

If you seek a dependable way to build an uncommon sales career, understand this fact: Rejection is an unavoidable part of the sales process. It is never to be taken personally.

An old adage reminds us that the sale doesn't really begin until the customer says "no." It's worth adding that your sales career doesn't really begin until you learn to accept "no" — and keep on selling.

The salesman frequently encounters the word "no." He must be resilient.

Robert W. Woodruff

Character consists of what you do on the third and fourth tries.

James A. Michener

Eighty-five percent of our customers
  say "no" at least once before buying.
  Ross Perot

Don't believe in defeat.
  Norman Vincent Peale

Ask yourself, "What's the worst
  that can happen?" Prepare to accept it.
  Then improve upon the worst.
  Dale Carnegie

The greatest test of courage on earth
  is to bear defeat without losing heart.
  Robert Ingersoll

Facing it — always facing it —that's the way
  to get through. Face it!
  Joseph Conrad

What is defeat? Nothing but education,
nothing but the first step to something better.
Wendell Phillips

There is no failure except
in no longer trying.
Elbert Hubbard

Good people are good because they've
come to wisdom through failure.
William Saroyan

To be successful, you've got to be willing
to fail.
Frank Tyger

Never let the fear of striking out
get in your way.
Babe Ruth

Never bend your head. Always hold it high.
Look the world straight in the face.
Helen Keller, speaking to a five-year-old blind child

All life is an experiment.
The more experiments you make, the better.
Ralph Waldo Emerson

Courage is the price that life extracts for
granting peace. The soul that knows it not
knows no release from little things.
Amelia Earhart

To conquer fear is the beginning of wisdom.
Bertrand Russell

Life begins on the other side of despair.
Jean-Paul Sartre

Despair is the conclusion of fools.

Benjamin Disraeli

Man is troubled not by things
    but by the view he takes of them.

Epictetus

In adversity, remember to keep an even mind.

Horace

Flowers grow out of dark moments.

Corita Kent

The road to valor is built by adversity.

Ovid

The school of hard knocks
    is an accelerated curriculum.

Menander

Troubles are often the tools by which God
fashions us for better things.

Henry Ward Beecher

Believe that for every problem
there is a solution.

Norman Vincent Peale

Make the most of your regrets.

Henry David Thoreau

That which does not kill me makes me stronger.

Friedrich Nietzsche

It is difficulties that show what men are.

Epictetus

Y‍ou gotta lose 'em sometimes.
When you do, lose 'em right!

Casey Stengel

A‍dversity? It's a tonic, not a stumbling block. Every adversity carries with it the seed of an equal or greater benefit.

Napoleon Hill

P‍roblems are the price of progress.
Don't bring me anything but trouble.
Good news weakens me.

Charles F. Kettering

T‍he turning point in the lives of those
who succeed, usually comes at the moment
of some crisis, through which they are
introduced to their "other selves."

Napoleon Hill

T‍he human spirit is stronger than anything
that can happen to it.

C. C. Scott

9

Optimism

Leo Tolstoy observed, "Faith is the force of life." Faith is also the force behind successful selling. The optimistic salesman conveys an attitude of confidence to the buyer. The result? Lots of closings. But the pessimist talks himself — and the customer — out of the sale. The result? Lots of frustrations.

If you're looking for a proven prescription to improve your closing ratios, try a healthy dose of optimism. Because if you think the sale will close — or think it won't — you're right.

Whenever a negative thought concerning
your personal power comes to mind,
deliberately voice a positive thought
to cancel it out.

Norman Vincent Peale

Fret not thyself.

Psalm 37:1

We can accomplish almost anything
within our ability if we but think we can!

George Matthew Adams

We would accomplish many more things
if we did not think of them as impossible.

C. Malesherbes

Sometimes success is due less to ability
than to zeal.

Charles Buxton

Our minds can shape the way a thing
will be because we act according
to our expectations.

Federico Fellini

They are able because they think
they are able.

Virgil

The greatest discovery is that a human being
can alter his life by altering his attitudes
of mind.

William James

We see things as *we* are, not as they are.

Leo Rosten

The sun shines not on us, but in us.

John Muir

There is one thing which gives radiance
to everything. It is the idea of something
around the corner.

C. K. Chesterton

All human wisdom is summed up
in two words — wait and hope.

Alexandre Dumas

Hope is a much greater stimulant of life
than any happiness.

Friedrich Nietzsche

They are ill discoverers who think there is
no land when they see nothing but sea.

Francis Bacon

The pessimist complains about the wind;
the optimist expects it to change;
the realist adjusts the sails.

William Arthur Ward

Optimism is the faith that leads
to achievement. Nothing can be done
without hope and confidence.

Helen Keller

A pessimist is one who makes difficulties
of his opportunities. An optimist is one who
makes opportunities of his difficulties.

Harry S. Truman

I am an optimist. It does not seem
too much use being anything else.

Sir Winston Churchill

Make optimism a way of life.

Lucille Ball

It doesn't hurt to be optimistic.
You can always cry later.

Lucimar Santos de Lima

Enthusiasm invites enthusiasm.

Russell Conwell

A man can succeed at almost anything
for which he has unlimited enthusiasm.

Charles M. Schwab

Great hopes make great men.

Thomas Fuller

The fearful Unbelief is unbelief in yourself.

Thomas Carlyle

Self-trust is the first secret of success.

Ralph Waldo Emerson

Enthusiasm is an inexhaustible source,
so mighty that you must ever tame and
temper it with wisdom.

Conrad Hilton

The trouble with the world is that the stupid
are cocksure and the intelligent
are full of doubt.

Bertrand Russell

It is often hard to distinguish between the
hard knocks in life and those of opportunity.

Frederick Phillips

When a man is willing and eager,
the gods join in.

Aeschylus

Whether you think you can or think you can't,
you're right.

Henry Ford

It is never too late
to be what you
might have been.

George Eliot

<u>10</u>

Thinking Big

Ralph Waldo Emerson wrote, "The world is all gates, all opportunities, strings of tension waiting to be struck." Emerson was a keenly gifted philosopher, but he spoke like a seasoned sales manager: He understood the power of big thoughts.

All of us are surrounded by a swirl of great opportunities, but we're usually too busy to notice. So we continue to do what we've always done, wondering why we get what we've always gotten.

If you're tired of the same old results, try a new approach: Make big plans; dream big dreams; and reach for the opportunities that surround you. In selling, big dreams *do* come true, but not until you dream them.

This is the true joy in life:
being used for a purpose
recognized by yourself
as a mighty one.

George Bernard Shaw

Think big. Act big.
Dream big.

Conrad Hilton

Do it big or stay in bed.

Larry Kelly

Whatever course you have chosen for
yourself, it will not be a chore but an
adventure if you bring to it a sense of the
glory of striving, if your sights are set far
above the merely secure and mediocre.

David Sarnoff

Every man is free to rise as far as he's able
or willing, but the degree to which he thinks
determines the degree to which he'll rise.

Ayn Rand

Real miracles are created by men
when they use their God-given courage
and intelligence.

Jean Anouilh

If you want a quality, act as if you already
have it.

William James

Learning is the discovery that something
is possible.

Fritz Perls

The only thing that stands between a man
and what he wants from life is often merely
the will to try it and the faith
to believe that it is possible.

Rich Devos

Ask yourself this question:
"How big can I dream?"

Conrad Hilton

Great things are not something accidental but must certainly be willed.

Vincent van Gogh

Sometimes, a big-ticket order must simmer. Don't rush a big order.

George M. Kahn

There is no security on this earth;
there is only opportunity.

General Douglas MacArthur

Impossibility is a word only to be found
in the dictionary of fools.

Napoléon I

I have learned to use the word *impossible*
with the greatest caution.

Wernher von Braun

Don't be afraid to take a big step if one
is indicated. You can't cross a chasm
in two small jumps.

David Lloyd George

As soon as you trust yourself,
you will know how to live.

Goethe

11

Time Management

Napoleon Hill observed, "Every man can surpass himself." This is especially true in the world of selling. Every salesman can surpass himself; to do so, he must learn to manage time.

In selling, there exists a subtle temptation to waste time. Sales calls, by their very nature, involve the possibility of rejection and disappointment. Often, it seems easier to shuffle papers than to sell, but beware: Excessive paper shuffling is invariably fatal to any sales career.

Brian Tracy advises salespeople to "ask yourself this question: Is what I'm doing right now going to lead to a sale?" If your answer is "no," then you must *make the time* for more sales calls. Because the Salesman's Hall of Fame is reserved for men and women who sell early and often ... no paper shufflers need apply.

Plan your work. Without a system,
you'll feel swamped.

Norman Vincent Peale

Time is your greatest asset:
Budget it carefully.

Napoleon Hill

The person who substitutes "now" for "later"
in his thinking succeeds best at selling.

Thomas J. Watson

Procrastination is the first enemy
of effective selling.

Brian Tracy

If a man would move the world,
he must first move himself.

Socrates

Drive thy business; let it not drive thee.

Ben Franklin

Take more time to think. And do things in the order of their importance.

Frank Bettger

To choose time is to save time.

Francis Bacon

We can't cross a bridge until we come to it, but I always like to lay down a pontoon ahead of time.

Bernard Baruch

Time is so precious that God deals it out only second by second.

Bishop Fulton J. Sheen

I owe all my success in life to having been always a quarter of an hour before my time.

Lord Nelson

Do the thing and you shall have the power.

Ralph Waldo Emerson

One cannot manage too many affairs;
like pumpkins in the water, one pops up while
you try to hold down the other.

Chinese Proverb

As you organize your life, you must
localize and define it. You cannot
do everything.

Phillips Brooks

Who begins too much accomplishes little.

German Proverb

There are people who want to be everywhere
at once, and they get nowhere.

Carl Sandburg

Look to today. Procrastination is the art
of keeping up with yesterday.

Don Marquis

If you lack peace of mind, you are not using your time to its best advantage.

Napoleon Hill

As a salesman, you must keep a reliable record of time, costs and results. Keep written records, then analyze them.

Thomas J. Watson

12

Continuing Education

A salesman's education is never completed; each day offers new opportunities to learn. Part of a salesman's training comes from nose-to-nose selling; in sales, there is no substitute for practical experience. But an integral part of one's training comes from books, tapes, sales meetings and courses.

If you intend to make a lifetime career in sales, make a lifetime commitment to learning. And never make the mistake of believing that you know everything there is to know about the art of selling. For the savvy salesman, school is always in session.

Selling is a skill, and like all skills, it must be learned through study and practice.

Thomas J. Watson

Only the most exceptional salespeople seek sales training. Only the best people invest in themselves.

Brian Tracy

Know your business and keep on knowing your business.

Frank Bettger

A salesman should never rationalize away sales failures. He should carefully analyze his approach and correct mistakes.

George M. Kahn

To learn is a natural pleasure, not confined to philosophers but common to all men.

Aristotle

Life is a festival only to the wise.

Ralph Waldo Emerson

Many receive advice, few profit by it.

Publilius Syrus

No man ever became wise by chance.

Seneca

As long as you live, keep learning how to live.

Seneca

Anyone who stops learning is old,
whether at twenty or eighty.

Henry Ford

The wish to progress is the largest part
of progress.

Seneca

What we are is God's gift to us.
What we become is our gift to God.

Eleanor Powell

Sales training should be a continuous process,
not a short-term "shot in the arm" program.

George M. Kahn

Observation, more than books, experience, rather than persons, are the prime educators.

A. B. Alcott

To imitate good models is a fine way to live.

Gilbert Highet

Learn from the skillful. He that teaches himself hath a fool for his master.

Ben Franklin

If you live with a lame man you will learn how to limp.

Plutarch

The wise learn many things from their foes.

Aristophanes

The most instructive experiences are those
of everyday life.

Friedrich Nietzsche

What we have to learn to do,
we learn by doing.

Aristotle

The doer alone learneth.

Friedrich Nietzsche

When the pupil is ready,
the teacher will come.

Chinese Saying

It's what you learn after you know it all
that counts.

Harry S. Truman

Only in growth,
reform, and change,
paradoxically enough,
is true security found.

Anne Morrow Lindbergh

When you're green,
you're growing;
when you're ripe,
you rot.

Ray Kroc

The essence of knowledge is, having it, to use it.

Confucius

13

All-Purpose Advice

We conclude with a potpourri of timely advice about the art of selling. Enjoy.

It's easier to explain price
one time than it is
to apologize for quality
forever.

Zig Ziglar

Find out where you can render a service;
then render it. The rest is up to the Lord.

S. S. Kresge

The most important secret of salesmanship
is to find out what the other fellow wants, then
help him find the best way to get it.

Frank Bettger

Don't hold out on life,
and life won't hold out on you.

Norman Vincent Peale

Give the customer dividends which he didn't figure on, and you'll have a friend for life.

Alfred E. Lyon

Never ignore a small order.
Little fish grow to be big fish.

George M. Kahn

Never run out of business cards.

Sales Adage

Everybody is a prospect.

Sales Adage

Learn to remember names.

Lyndon B. Johnson

Get absolutely enthralled with something.
Throw yourself into it with abandon.
Get out of yourself. Be somebody.
Do something.

Norman Vincent Peale

It is up to you to live the life the Creator
gave you.

Napoleon Hill

The world belongs to the energetic.

Ralph Waldo Emerson

Fortune favors the bold but abandons
the timid.

Latin Proverb

Keep away from people who try to belittle
your ambitions.

Mark Twain

Truth is always exciting. Speak it, then.
Life is dull without it.

Pearl Buck

A man's character is his fate.

Heraclitus

What is success? I think it is a mixture of
having a flair for the thing that you are doing
and working with a sense of purpose.

Margaret Thatcher

Think like a man of action,
and act like a man of thought.

Henri Bergson

There is nothing so useless as doing efficiently
what should not be done at all.

Peter Drucker

None will improve your lot if you yourselves
do not.

Bertolt Brecht

Freedom is the supreme good — freedom
from self-imposed limitations.

Elbert Hubbard

The tragedy of life is not so much what men
suffer but what they miss.

Thomas Carlyle

At least ten times every day affirm this
thought, "I expect the best and,
with God's help, will attain the best."

Norman Vincent Peale

May you live all the days of your life.

Jonathan Swift

Resolve to be thyself; and know
that he who finds himself loses his misery.
Matthew Arnold

Too many people overvalue what they're not
and undervalue what they are.
Malcolm Forbes

In order to be irreplaceable,
one must be different.
Coco Chanel

Learn what you are and be such.
Pindar

Always aim for achievement, and forget
about success.
Helen Hayes

Marketing and innovation produce results.
All the rest are costs.

Peter Drucker

Try new ideas by doing new things.
Inject newness into the daily routine.

Stanley Marcus

New business is the lifeblood
of your company.

Ross Perot

In the business world, everyone is paid
in two coins: cash and experience. Take the
experience first; the cash will come later.

Harold Geneen

Your prospect is not going to buy cold hard
facts. He is going to buy warm people benefits.

Zig Ziglar

Opportunity knocks
once at every man's door
and then keeps
on knocking.

George Ade

Sources

Sources

Sources

Louis Pasteur 98
Anna Pavolva 53
Norman Vincent Peale 32, 38,
    81, 85, 104, 109, 112, 128,
    147, 149, 151, 153
William Penn 92
Fritz Perls 123
Ross Perot 21, 80, 88, 104,
    153
Persius 93
Tom Peters 70, 75
Frederick Phillips 117
Wendell Phillips 105
Pindar 152
Plutarch 140
Poor Richard's Almanac 47,
    48
Eleanor Powell 139
Ptahhotep 64
Publilius Syrus 65, 138
Ayn Rand 122
Charles Revson 79
Eleanor Roosevelt 75
Pete Rose 37
Leo Rosten 113
John Ruskin 45, 84, 96
Bertrand Russell 40, 106, 117
Babe Ruth 98, 105
Carl Sandburg 132
Harland Sanders 54
David Sarnoff 64, 122
William Saroyan 105
Jean-Paul Sartre 106
Vidal Sassoon, 42
Ruth Ann Schabacker 22
Charles M. Schwab 16, 116
C. C. Scott 110
Seneca 38, 65, 138, 139
William Shakespeare 37, 61
George Bernard Shaw 58, 120
Fulton J. Sheen 131
Robert L. Shook 78

Alfred E. Smith 85
Socrates 128
Sylvester Stallone 94
Casey Stengel 110
Robert Louis Stevenson 17,
    29
W. Clement Stone 25
Igor Stravinsky 83
Jonathan Swift 153
Walter LeMar Talbot 88
Terence 36, 65
Margaret Thatcher 152
Henry David Thoreau 61,
    109
J. R. R. Tolkien 50
Leo Tolstoy 111
Brian Tracy 19, 60, 89, 127,
    128, 137
Anthony Trollope 24
Harry S. Truman 115, 141
Mark Twain 149
Frank Tyger 105
Paul Valéry 64
Virgil 113
W. W. Wager 59
William Arthur Ward 28, 39,
    114
Thomas J. Watson 19, 57,
    77, 80, 100, 128, 134, 136
Woodrow Wilson 74
Robert W. Woodruff 80, 102
Zig Ziglar 30, 32, 78, 86, 146,
    153

About the Author

Criswell Freeman is a Doctor of Clinical Psychology living in Nashville, Tennessee. He is the author of *When Life Throws You a Curveball, Hit It* and numerous books in the Wisdom Series published by WALNUT GROVE PRESS.

Dr. Freeman's Wisdom Books chronicle memorable quotations in an easy-to-read style. The series provides inspiring, thoughtful and humorous messages from entertainers, athletes, scientists, politicians, clerics, writers and renegades, with each title focusing on a particular region or area of special interest. Combining his passion for quotations with extensive training in psychology, Freeman revisits timeless themes such as perseverance, courage, love, forgiveness and faith.

Dr. Freeman is also the host of *Wisdom Made in America*, a nationally syndicated radio program.

The Wisdom Series
by Dr. Criswell Freeman

Regional Titles

Wisdom Made in America	ISBN 1-887655-07-7
The Book of Southern Wisdom	ISBN 0-9640955-3-X
The Wisdom of the Midwest	ISBN 1-887655-17-4
The Wisdom of the West	ISBN 1-887655-31-X
The Book of Texas Wisdom	ISBN 0-9640955-8-0
The Book of Florida Wisdom	ISBN 0-9640955-9-9
The Book of California Wisdom	ISBN 1-887655-14-X
The Book of New York Wisdom	ISBN 1-887655-16-6
The Book of New England Wisdom	ISBN 1-887655-15-8

Sports Titles

The Golfer's Book of Wisdom	ISBN 0-9640955-6-4
The Putter Principle	ISBN 1-887655-39-5
The Golfer's Guide to Life	ISBN 1-887655-38-7
The Wisdom of Women's Golf	ISBN 1-887655-82-4
The Book of Football Wisdom	ISBN 1-887655-18-2
The Wisdom of Southern Football	ISBN 0-9640955-7-2
The Book of Stock Car Wisdom	ISBN 1-887655-12-3
The Wisdom of Old-Time Baseball	ISBN 1-887655-08-5
The Book of Basketball Wisdom	ISBN 1-887655-32-8
The Fisherman's Guide to Life	ISBN 1-887655-30-1
The Tennis Lover's Guide to Life	ISBN 1-887655-36-0

Special People Titles

Mothers Are Forever	ISBN 1-887655-76-X
Fathers Are Forever	ISBN 1-887655-77-8
Friends Are Forever	ISBN 1-887655-78-6
The Teacher's Book of Wisdom	ISBN 1-887655-80-8
The Graduate's Book of Wisdom	ISBN 1-887655-81-6
The Guide to Better Birthdays	ISBN 1-887655-35-2
Get Well Soon...If Not Sooner	ISBN 1-887655-79-4
The Wisdom of the Heart	ISBN 1-887655-34-4

Special Interest Titles

The Book of Country Music Wisdom	ISBN 0-9640955-1-3
Old-Time Country Wisdom	ISBN 1-887655-26-3
The Wisdom of Old-Time Television	ISBN 1-887655-64-6
The Book of Cowboy Wisdom	ISBN 1-887655-41-7
The Gardener's Guide to Life	ISBN 1-887655-40-9
The Salesman's Book of Wisdom	ISBN 1-887655-83-2
Minutes from the Great Women's Coffee Club (by Angela Beasley)	ISBN 1-887655-33-6

Wisdom Books are available at fine stores everywhere.
For information about a retailer near you, call toll-free 1-888-WISE GIFT.